Objects of Desire

SHEILA METZNER ▪ PHOTOGRAPHS

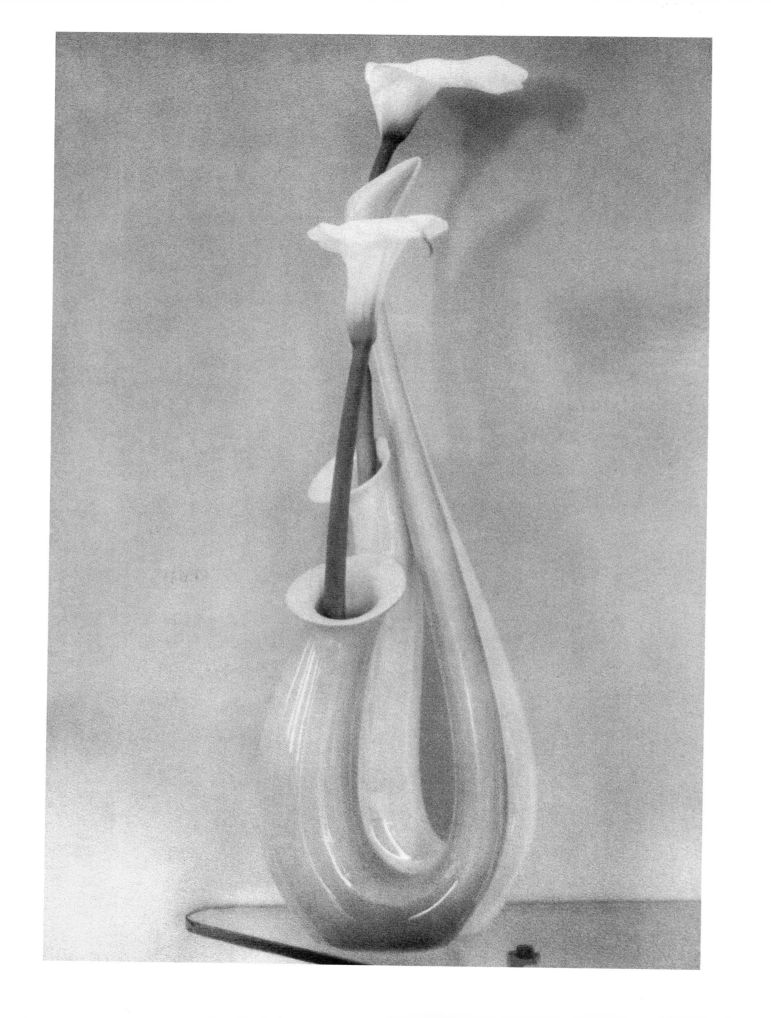

Objects of Desire

SHEILA METZNER ▪ PHOTOGRAPHS

PREFACE BY MARK STRAND

A POLAROID BOOK

CLARKSON N. POTTER, INC./PUBLISHERS

DISTRIBUTED BY CROWN PUBLISHERS, INC., NEW YORK

Prepared and produced by the Publications Department of Polaroid Corporation, and published by Clarkson N. Potter, Inc., 225 Park Avenue South, New York, New York 10003.

CLARKSON N. POTTER, POTTER, and colophon are trademarks of Clarkson N. Potter, Inc.

Manufactured in the United States of America

Library of Congress Cataloging-in-Publication Data

Metzner, Sheila.
  Objects of desire.

  "A Polaroid book."
  1. Photography, Artistic. 2. Metzner, Sheila.
1. Strand, Mark 1934-   . II. Title.
TR654.M4636   1986   779'.092'4   86-3220
ISBN 0-517-56234-0

10 9 8 7 6 5 4 3 2 1

First Edition

Frontispiece: SAXOPHONE VASE WITH CALLAS • 1985
Front cover: JOKO PASSION • 1985
        Courtesy of ULTRA magazine, April 1985
Back cover: HOMAGE TO MAN RAY • 1983

Printed by Acme Printing Company, Medford, Massachusetts, and bound by Publishers Book Bindery, Long Island City, New York.

For my mother, Helen, who inspired "desire."

To my husband Jeffrey, the hero of this fiction, and to our children

Raven, Bega, Ruby, Stella, Louie, and Alison and Evyan.

Preface

A strange light inhabits Sheila Metzner's photographs, a kind of airy amber that cannot be associated with a time of day. It caresses rather than illuminates. It is secret and maternal; it touches everything but exposes nothing. It is a preserving light, a warmth, a glow. Nothing is lost in it.

Objects seem to drift from one photograph to another. A red fabric with white dots scattered over it covers a round tabletop in one, while in another it is a backdrop, a red sky in which dozens of moons seem to float. There are flowers everywhere, and Art Deco vases, and sculpture, and postcard reproductions of paintings, and even photographs, each object proclaiming its own exquisite immobility and disclosing something of the privileged lair about the interiors. In one background there is a large Francis Frith photograph of a pyramid and the sphinx. To one side there is a sconce that looks like a badminton bird stylized into angularity. A masked seminude female lies on a daybed, lightly clutching herself. Two red pillows rise at the same angle behind her, a satin spread coils in front. But she is oblivious to these suggestions of rhythm and allusions to near and distant past. She is already adrift in the remote reaches of a personal lethargy.

Sheila Metzner's subjects appear fatigued by self-possession, and livened, paradoxically, by a yearning for relief from the physical and forgettable, each of them drawn to routines of timelessness, to some miraculous absence that increases immeasurably, invisibly, from within. They lean or lie back, drape or stretch themselves. They wear costumes that enhance the body's presence as a chic and sensuous preserve. There is a feline fluency about their descent into stillness. And though the expressions of their surrender are caught by the

SELF-PORTRAIT · 1981

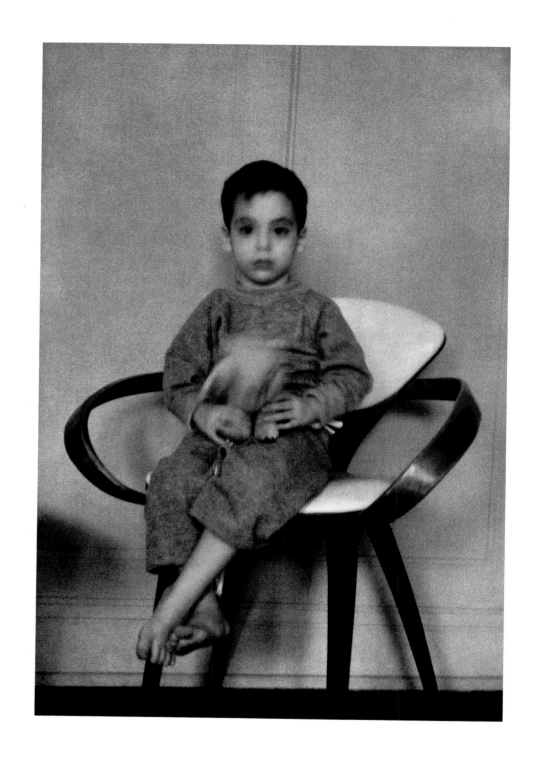

LOUIE • 1984

JEFFREY, RED SHIRT · 1980

RAVEN ASLEEP • 1984

DANIEL WOLF · 1979

camera, there is little in the photograph that could be construed as overtly sexual; rather what we see is the theatrical surround of sexuality, decor that hints at the erotic. In one photograph a dark-haired woman, her eyes closed and her head turned to the side and tilted slightly back, seems on the point of being ravished as the beaklike spout of a pitcher reaches up to her lips. But, like the woman on the daybed, she is already in another world. Her languor has etherealized her, so that the photograph, despite its suggestion of Leda and the Swan, is in fact a portrayal of seduction denied. She appears to have abandoned herself only to the camera's extraordinary power to push back the tides of transience.

In these photographs there is no compromise with the urgent or the timely, with the accidental or the candid. In fact, there are no events in the work but the photographic ones that insure stability or permanence. This world is a staged world, a world of stilled life. There is something tomblike about it, something faintly Egyptian in the postures that the subjects assume, with their shoulders usually positioned frontally before the camera as they bask in the soothing solitudes of their particular desires. They have their eternal postures, not in the conventional or predictable domain of photographic portraiture but in the realm where the passion of photographic portraiture is enacted—in that blissful instant of change when they become, without hesitancy, objects of desire. Privacy is never violated; it is given over. The photographer's subjects all seem to say "take me," as if they knew that surrender meant deliverance, that their gestures of relinquishment would preserve them.   MARK STRAND

BEGA, EVYAN, AND RUBY ASLEEP • 1975

EVYAN • 1975

BEGA, CHATHAM • 1981

STELLA BY STARLIGHT • 1982

EVYAN, GOLDEN GIRL • 1982

BEGA, STILL LIFE WITH PEPPERS • 1982

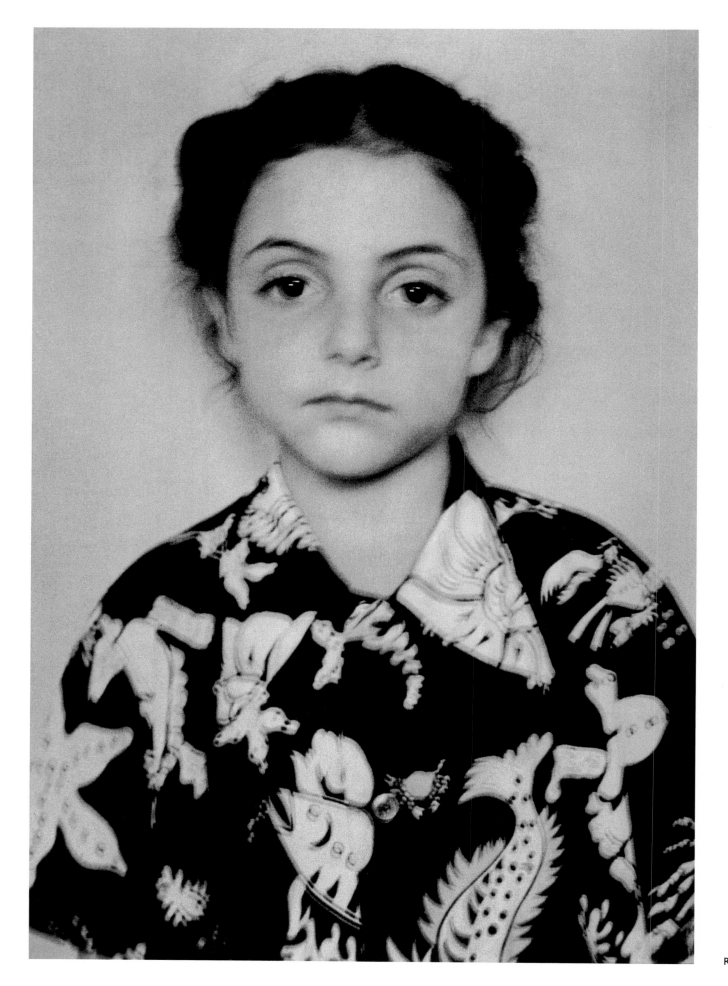

RUBY, MIAMI SHIRT · 1980

RUBY, TULIPS • 1980

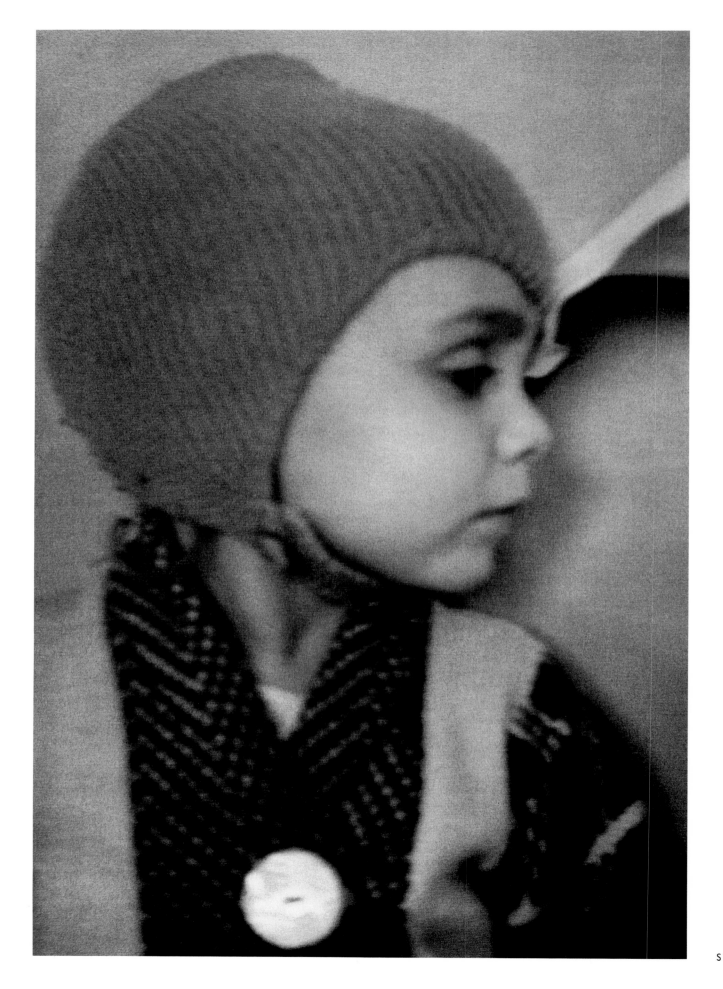

STELLA, CALLA • 1980

BEGA, PLASTIC HAT • 1983

MICHAL, BREAST · 1980

MICHAL, ODALISQUE • 1980

BLACK-AND-WHITE STILL LIFE IN COLOR • 1984

SNOW FALLING • 1985

MICHAL, DREAM · 1980

WHITE ANTHURIUMS FOR

JEANNE MOREAU • 1984

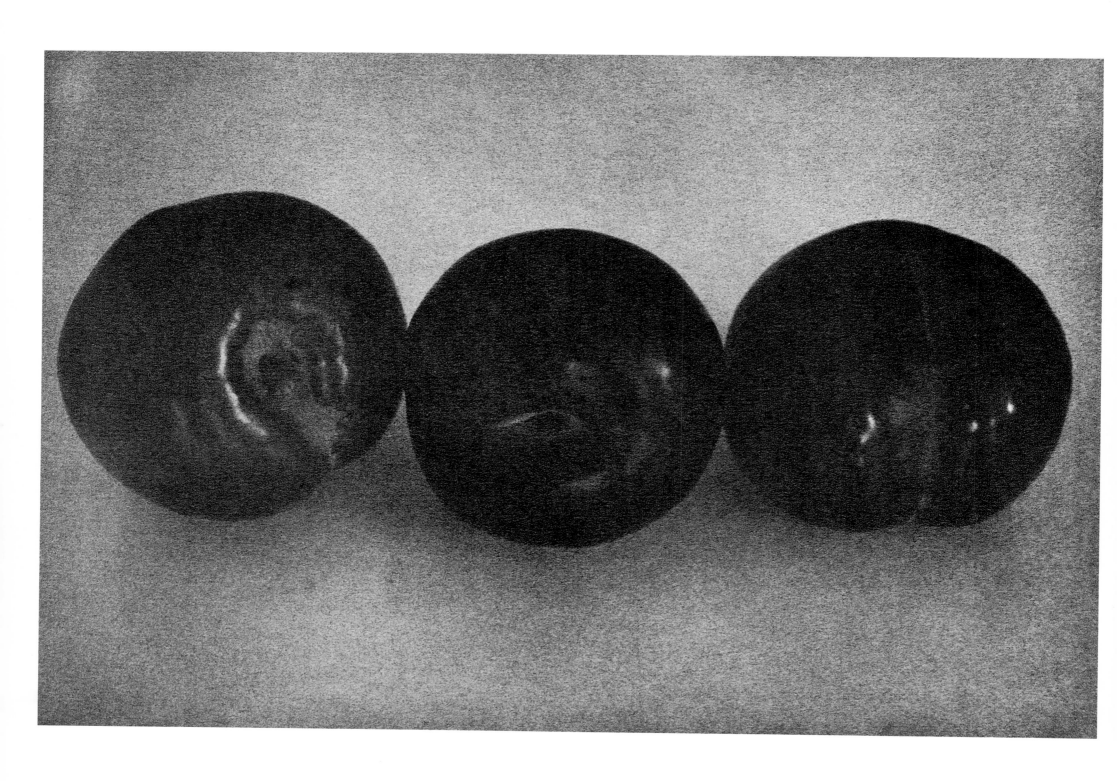

THREE PLUMS · 1981

MONDRIAN ORCHID · 1982

GRAY VASE, VANDA ORCHID · 1980

HOMAGE TO

MAN RAY • 1983

MICHAL, HAT • 1980

VASE, SIXTH FLOOR • 1980

JOHN, BLACK SHIRT • 1980

LISA KALFUS,
RED JUMPSUIT · 1980

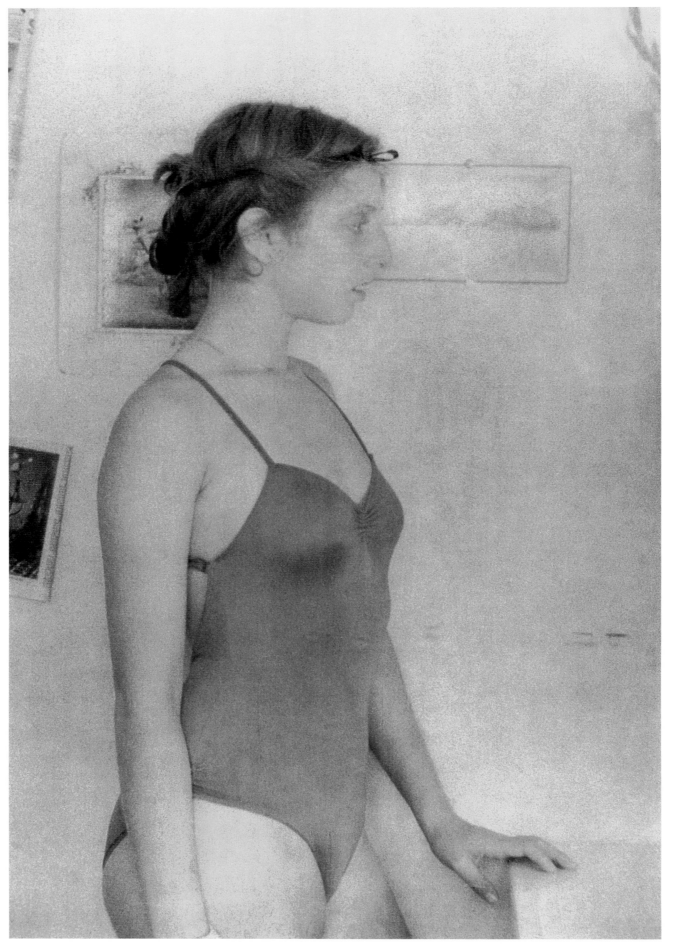

ALISON,
BATHING SUIT · 1981

JAPANESE STILL LIFE • 1982

JOHN SAYLES • 1983

JOHN SAYLES

IN OUR BEDROOM · 1983

CARLOTTA · 1985

ANDRÉE PUTMAN · 1984

JEANNE MOREAU • 1983

JOHN HUSTON AT HOME
IN LAS CALETAS · 1983

JILL IN OUR BEDROOM • 1984

ROSEMARY,
UNGARO HAT • 1985

JANIE PARKER, BALLERINA • 1984

JOKO, RED VALENTINO

DRESS • 1985

UMA, PATOU DRESS
AND HAT • 1986

ARNOLD STEINHARDT

(VIOLIN) · 1982

LAETITIA, ARP • 1985

REBECCA WITH MARLO'S FLOWERS • 1984

REBECCA, DIAMOND NECKLACE • 1984

JOKO PASSION • 1985

REBECCA, GOLDFISH • 1985

ART DECO • 1984

ROSIMA · 1985

UMA • 1985

BORNEO GIRL • 1985

DUNAND VASE · 1983

MOUILLE STILL LIFE • 1985

Acknowledgments

I would like to express my appreciation to Constance Sullivan, who gave this book its being. Thanks also to Alexander Liberman, Condé Nast Publications Inc., Grace Mirabella, Anna Wintour, Polly Mellen, Diana Edkins, Lloyd Ziff, Mary Shanahan, Ruth Ansel, Elisabeth Biondi, Paul Sinclaire and Grace Coddington; to Aaron Rose; to Lou Dorfsman; to Weston Naef and John Szarkowski; to Daniel Wolf, Inc. and the G. Ray Hawkins Gallery; to friends who sit for me, provide sets, props, and wardrobe: Anthony DeLorenzo, Steven Greenberg, Galerie Metropol, D. Leonard & Gerry Trent, Barry Friedman, Ltd., Fifty-50, Modernism, Audrey Friedman and Chaim Manishevitz; to Madderlake for flowers, Gerard Bollei and Didier Malige for hair, and Linda Mason, Kevyn Aucoin and Michelle Voyski for make-up; to Katy Homans and Scott Hyde; and to Nell Gutman, my studio manager, and Rick DiNome, my production manager. I will always be grateful for the strong relationships that have evolved from our working together.

SHEILA METZNER

Credits

OBJECTS OF DESIRE

was edited by Constance Sullivan.

Editorial preparation and production

were coordinated by Abigail Hutchinson.

Production was supervised by Robert McVoy.

The book was designed by Katy Homans.